Newborn Movement Assessment™

Newborn Movement Assessment™

THE EVALUATION AND STIMULATION OF AN INFANT'S DEVELOPMENTAL MOVEMENTS

. . .

Michelle Turner
Creator of Movement Lesson™

ISBN: 0692578714
ISBN 13: 9780692578711

The Newborn Movement Assessment™ is not intended to be a substitute for the medical advice of physicians. The reader should regularly consult a physician in matters relating to their infant's health, particularly with respect to any symptoms that may require diagnosis or medical attention.

The intent of the Newborn Movement Assessment™ is for parents and professionals to understand that initiating movement patterns immediately or within days of birth will lead to optimal cognitive development. Sound medical decisions should continually be made for each infant. The Newborn Movement Assessment™ is not critical of delivery choices or medical evaluations. Rather, it is designed to be complementary to assessments already in place, such as the Apgar Score.

Table of Contents

About Michelle Turner and Movement Lesson™

• • •

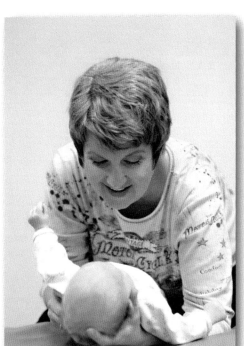

OUT OF NECESSITY TO HELP her globally delayed child, Michelle Turner, Movement Integration Specialist, created Movement Lesson™ to benefit children throughout the world. Founded in 2009, Movement Lesson™, LLC is a private practice located in Peoria, Arizona, USA, and is dedicated to helping children from ages 0 – 94 achieve increased mobility, pain relief, and optimal health. In contrast to the myriad of conventional therapies, a Movement Lesson™ is a progressive, scientific approach that is based on her theory of the opposition of gravity and principles of movement affecting development. More specifically, a Movement Lesson™ utilizes a unique combination of gentle touch and purposeful movement through the principles of counterbalance and rotation to create an individualized and profoundly effective movement lesson session.

Introduction to the Newborn Movement Assessment

• • •

WELCOME TO THE NEWBORN MOVEMENT Assessment™ (NMA) Guide. This guide intends to give parents and professionals the opportunity to assess an infant's movements from birth throughout their first year of life. Presently, there are medical and genetic tests to assist, coordinate, and direct an infant's doctors and nurses in order to identify current and potential health concerns. In contrast, the Newborn Movement Assessment™ introduces an effective comprehensive guide to determine short-term and long-term developmental concerns, and also optimize, and stimulate the baby's movement patterns through gentle touch. The Newborn Movement Assessment™ is a tool for assessing any baby's typical or atypical birth experience.

The necessity for early detection and intervention is clearly evident in the growing prevalence of developmental concerns such as autism, cerebral palsy, and genetic disorders. Without this crucial early intervention program, infants exhibiting movement concerns are at a much higher risk of having long-term special needs. These techniques will result in immediate improvements to an infant's development, whether the infant is completely healthy or demonstrating significant developmental delays. Ultimately, the objective of the Newborn Movement Assessment™ is to demonstrate that initiating specific movement patterns at birth or shortly afterwards will encourage optimal cognitive and motor development.

B.R.I.G.H.T. Principles

. . .

THE NEWBORN MOVEMENT ASSESSMENT™ HAS been developed to introduce movement patterns, enhance movement experiences, and create proactive parents and professionals. This is the first assessment guide with step-by-step instructions on how to enhance your baby's development. There are three easy steps to evaluate a baby's **B.R.I.G.H.T.** future:

- Evaluate the **B**irthing Process
- Assess the **R**otation
- **I**nitiate a **G**entle **H**ealthy **T**ouch.

It's that simple: **B** - Birth, **R**- Rotation, **IGHT** - Initiate Gentle Healthy Touch.

By implementing the Newborn Movement Assessment's **B.R.I.G.H.T.** principles, you will not only begin to understand this natural language of movement, but also begin to evolve this language into new and purposeful movement patterns. One purpose of the Newborn Movement Assessment™ program is to empower parents and professionals to become active participants in an infant's movement vocabulary.

The Evaluation of Birth and Rotation

. . .

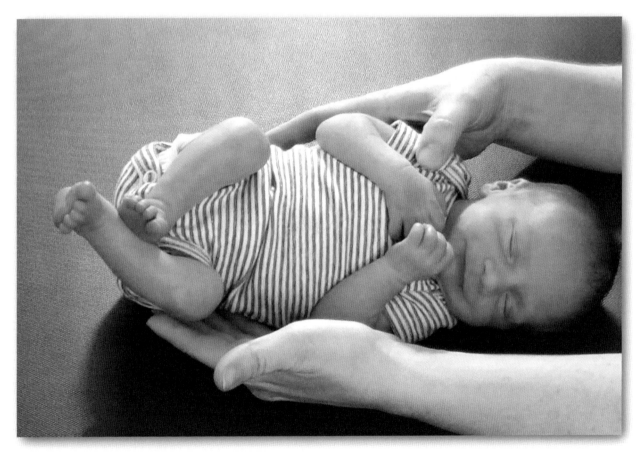

Evaluation ofbirth

. . .

Significance of Natural Birth

A FULL-TERM VAGINAL DELIVERY IS a key in the development of the baby's central nervous system. One of the primary purposes of a vaginal delivery is to initiate rotation in a newborn's central nervous system and also, to stimulate the brain's ability to learn from movement and environmental stimulation. Bypassing this process, due to medical complications or genetics, may result in a baby unable to respond to stimuli or to move typically.

---

central nervous system: noun
the part of the nervous system comprising the brain and spinal cord.

The intent is for a baby to come into this world through a natural delivery. During the delivery, the baby will start a very slow rotation as the head presents and is helped out of the vaginal canal. This process has

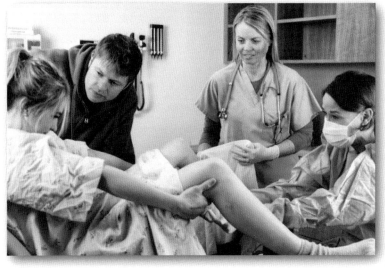

the added element of contractions, which prepares the baby's body to associate itself with the gravitational force that launches organ function, the lungs being the most obvious. Immediately, after the head presents, there is the bearing down of pressure through the upper chest cavity to empty and set up the lungs for their first breath while the diaphragm responds by billowing for air intake. This is one example in which underweight babies can be deficit in the birthing experience. The size of the mother's vaginal canal in coordination with the size of the child affects the force of the torque through the birthing process. At this point, there are medical options available for the baby's delivery.

Torque: noun
a twisting force that tends to cause rotation.

Rotation: noun
The act or process of turning through parts or all of the human body to create a transformation of a co-ordinate system in a sequence or series.

IMPACT OF MEDICATIONS

There are several considerations concerning the mother and the unborn baby if a medicated delivery is necessary. Medications or anesthetics are nerve blocks that interrupt the neural pathways which carry sensations of pain to the brain. Many professionals do not explain the possible side effects that a medicated childbirth has on a newborn's ability to move and react immediately after birth. Moderate to severe reactions from medications can affect newborn babies and may include the inability to suck or issues with breathing that lead to time spent in the Neonatal Intensive Care Unit (NICU). For most babies these effects gradually improve and an infant's ability or inability to move can be determined with the Newborn Movement Assessment™.

IMPACT OF SURGICAL DELIVERIES

A pregnancy that is unable to deliver a baby naturally through the birth canal (vaginal birth) due to possible medical complications is either pre-planned or an emergency cesarean section (C-section). A C-section is often scheduled prior to the delivery date due to preeclampsia, hypertension or a prior C-section. Other reasons for a planned C-section are a high-risk infant delivering with known birth defects to the organs, or in cases of multiple births. No one wants to put a child at risk but there are concerns among doctors about

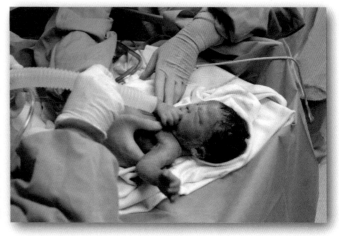

liability issues surrounding the birthing process. The World Health Organization has projected that most countries have a cesarean-section rate of no more than 15%. In the United States, fifty years ago, 1 out of 20 births were from a C-section. The current rate for a C-section is 1 out of 3 births.

Movement trauma, which affects a newborn's natural movement patterns, increases as interventions to delivery increase. The simple act of pulling a baby out of the uterus without any purposeful rotation can fail to stimulate the central nervous system, limiting the ability of the baby to react to stimuli, and therefore, limits the newborn's ability to respond to the environment.

Evaluation of Rotation

· · ·

IMPORTANCE OF ROTATION

ONE OF THE MOST IMPORTANT features of the Newborn Movement Assessment™ is its ability to identify an infant's lack of rotation immediately following birth. Rotation is crucial in order to set up the central nervous system and establish the newborn's orientation to gravity. When an infant is unable to rotate correctly, he is then unable to oppose gravity, and is likely to have developmental delays and challenges with such activities as sitting and walking. The Newborn Movement Assessment™ gives parents and professionals new tools to improve an infant's reaction to stimuli, and therefore, increase his capacity to thrive and develop.

All learning and development is due to or through rotation and torque. If a person develops typically with no delays, but traumatizes the rotation and torque in their system, that body system guarantees pain and other complications. When a baby cannot rotate, or his ability to rotate becomes traumatized, the baby cannot oppose gravity, as in sitting up. All humans oppose gravity, which is the ability to walk upright and with continuous movements. When the response of gravity in a baby's system supersedes the ability to respond, the infant is unable to thrive.

A baby, unable to react to stimuli and who lies in one place, is held only in a specific position, or who can only move in a particular pattern, has and will continue to have special needs. The behavior of reacting to a light, touching a ball, tasting a mother's breast milk, or smelling their father's cologne, stimulates the central nervous system to continue developing. The compilation of millions of these developmental movements will create neuropathways and increase cognitive development. The less a baby moves or reacts, the fewer options that child will have for typical reactions to stimuli.

Newborn Movement Assessment™ Evaluation

· · ·

THE NEWBORN MOVEMENT ASSESSMENT™ EVALUATION can be completed while the newborn is awake or asleep. It is recommended for newborns to be lying on their backs to conduct the assessment. You can set up a phone or video camera to record your thoughts and observations as you evaluate your child.

The following areas of the infant's body will be addressed during the assessment: head, shoulders, arms/elbows, hands/wrists, pelvis, spine, chest, legs/knees, and feet/ankles. The complexities of the human body will become clearer as each area of the infant's body is examined. Please watch the following video, located at www.newbornmovementassessment.com, before you proceed with a Newborn Movement Assessment™.

The Newborn Movement Assessment™ is not intended to be a substitute for the medical advice of physicians. The reader should regularly consult a physician in matters relating to their infant's health, particularly with respect to any symptoms that may require diagnosis or medical attention.

HEAD

INTRODUCTION TO THE HEAD
The head is one of the most important body parts to view the initial qualities of movement since most of the senses are in the head. Most of the topical senses (sound, taste, smell, and sight) reside in the heads ability to respond to the environment. The head requires equal opportunities for movement to the left and right during the first year of life. Just as there is no hand dominance, there should be no dominance for head movement.

ASSESSMENT DIRECTIONS FOR THE HEAD
Gently slide your fingers underneath the head. Slightly tilt the head to the left and then to the right. You are not trying to touch the infant's ear to the shoulder. This is a slight movement in which you are looking for a response, not a result. Gently place the infant's head back on the crib mattress. Watch the infant rest.

Please watch the video below and consider the following questions while conducting the assessment:

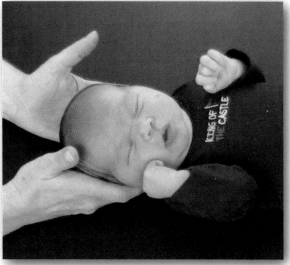

- Do you notice that you cannot move the head to the right but you can to the left?
- Do you notice if the infant's head is asymmetrical while lying down?
- Does the infant's head or nose face one foot or one shoulder?
- Does the same side shoulder and pelvis present with less rotation?

If you have answered yes to any of these questions, please place a "1" under the head section of the Newborn Movement Assessment™ Evaluation Sheet. Please contact your child's pediatrician immediately if you have any medical concerns.

SHOULDERS

INTRODUCTION TO THE SHOULDERS

Movement through the shoulders is the key to crawling and presenting onto all fours. The shoulders work in tandem with counterbalance and the ability to reach and touch objects.

ASSESSMENT DIRECTIONS FOR THE SHOULDERS

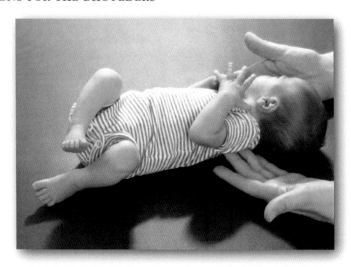

Gently slide one to two fingers under the right shoulder with a light lift. In most cases, the width of your two fingers will be enough depending on the size of the child. Now slide one to two fingers under the left shoulder with a light lift. Gently place the infant's shoulders back on the crib mattress. Watch the infant rest. Please watch the video below and consider the following questions while conducting the assessment:

- Was it easy to lift both shoulders?
- Did you notice that both arms responded by going in and out of a bent position?
- Did you notice a significant difference from lifting the right side in comparison to the left?
- Did the infant's head respond only to the movement in one shoulder?
- Were one or both arms stiff or straight?
- Were one or both arms floppy or non-responsive?
- Follow-up with your pediatrician if you have other concerns.

If you have answered yes to any of these questions, please place a "1" under the shoulder section of the Newborn Movement Assessment™ Evaluation Sheet. Please follow-up with your pediatrician immediately if you have any medical concerns.

Arms/Elbows

Introduction to the Arms/Elbows
The elbows are early indicators of how the body can respond to being on and off the floor in response to a healthy opposition to gravity.

Assessment Directions for the Arms/Elbows
Gently slide your hand under the right elbow. As you lift the elbow, notice if the arm is moving and is bending in and out. When touching or picking up the elbow, focus on rotating, not bending, gently through the mid-arm. Gently place the infant's elbow back on the flat surface. Repeat the same assessment on the left elbow. Please watch the video below and consider the following questions while conducting the assessment:

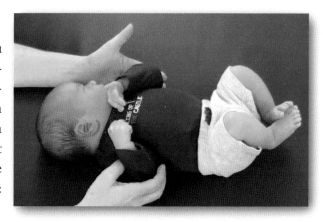

- Was it easy to lift both elbows?
- Was it easy to rotate the arms/elbows?
- Is there a difference in rotation from the left in comparison to the right?

If you have answered yes to any of these questions, please place a "1" under the arms/elbows section of the Newborn Movement Assessment™ Evaluation Sheet. Please follow-up with your pediatrician immediately if you have any medical concerns.

Wrists/Hands

Introduction to the Hands
The beginning movements of the hands are the window to fine motor skills that will be needed for daily tasks. The simple act of opening and closing the hands show simple muscle response that is needed to respond to stimuli.

Assessment Directions for the Hands
Gently lift your infant's hand into your fingers. Gently rotate their hand through the palm and the wrist to the right and to the left. Let their hand rest to their side and watch for movement. Continue to watch the video as needed and consider the following questions while conducting the assessment:

- Is there a difference in rotation from the left in comparison to the right?
- Is it hard to open the hand?
- Do the fingers move in and out around you?
- If there are movement concerns, is there rotation in each finger?
- Does the infant startle or panic?

If you have answered yes to any of these questions, please place a "1" under the hand section of the Newborn Movement Assessment™ Evaluation Sheet. Please follow-up with your pediatrician immediately if you have any medical concerns.

SPINE

INTRODUCTION TO THE SPINE

The twist or rotation of the spine is an indicator of the health and flexibility of the body.

ASSESSMENT DIRECTIONS FOR THE SPINE

Gently rotate your child to their side. Gently rotate the child's pelvis to the forward and backwards. Gently place the infant's back on the crib mattress. Watch the infant rest. Please watch the video below and consider the following questions while conducting the assessment:

- Is there a difference in rotation going forwards or backwards?
- Is it easy for the body to go with the movement?
- Does the infant startle or panic?
- Does the infant seem stiff or is it hard to rotate through the spine?
- Does the infant seem soft or non-responsive to rotation?
- Does the infant seem to fall or flop?

If you have answered yes to any of these questions, please place a "1" under the spine section of the Newborn Movement Assessment™ Evaluation Sheet. Please follow-up with your pediatrician immediately if you have any medical concerns.

CHEST

INTRODUCTION TO THE CHEST

The ability for any baby's chest rotation is not only a healthy indicator for breathing but quickly develops into rolling over and sitting up.

ASSESSMENT DIRECTIONS FOR THE CHEST

Gently touch your infant's chest as if you were checking on how they are breathing. Gently rotate the chest to the right and to the left. Gently let your infant rest lying on their back. Watch the infant rest. Please watch the video below and consider the following questions while conducting the assessment:

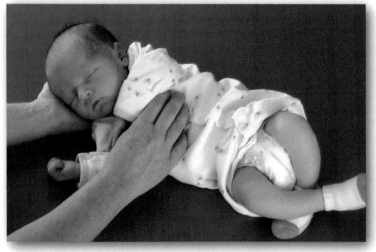

- Is there a difference in rotation from the left in comparison to the right?
- Do you feel rotation in the chest?
- Does the infant seem stiff or is it hard to rotate through the chest?
- Does the infant seem soft or non-responsive to rotation?
- Does the infant startle, panic or seem to stop breathing?
- Does the infant seem to fall or flop?

If you have answered yes to any of these questions, please place a "1" under the chest section of the Newborn Movement Assessment™ Evaluation Sheet. Please follow-up with your pediatrician immediately if you have any medical concerns.

PELVIS

INTRODUCTION TO THE PELVIS

An infant's pelvis is the key for coordination from the spine to the brain/skull. Later you will be able to see the significance of pelvic movement in crawling, learning how to get up and down and walking.

ASSESSMENT DIRECTIONS FOR THE PELVIS

Gently slide one to two fingers under the right pelvis with a light lift. In most cases, the width of your two fingers will be enough of a lift depending on the size of the infant. Now, slide one to two fingers under the left pelvis with a light lift. Gently place the infant's pelvis back on the flat surface. Watch the infant rest. Please watch the video below and consider the following questions while conducting the assessment:

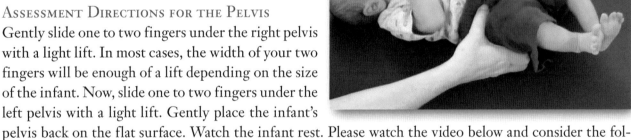

- Was it easy to lift both sides of the pelvis?
- Did you notice that both legs responded by going in and out of a bent position?
- Did you notice a significant difference from lifting the right side in comparison to the left?
- Were one or both legs stiff or straight?
- Were one or both legs floppy or non-responsive?

If you have answered yes to any of these questions, please place a "1" under the pelvis section of the Newborn Movement Assessment™ Evaluation Sheet. Please follow-up with your pediatrician immediately if you have any medical concerns.

LEGS/KNEES

INTRODUCTION TO THE LEGS/KNEES

The ways in which the knees bend and rotate are indicators of how the infant will bring his knees to the floor in crawling. A baby's leg should spring as it goes in and out extending and bending.

ASSESSMENT DIRECTIONS FOR THE LEGS/KNEES

Gently slide your hand under the right knee. As you lift the knee, notice if the leg gently bends or if the leg stays straight. There is a difference between a leg that goes in and out and a leg engaging in a bend. Lightly hold the thigh through the femur (thigh) and rotate your hand left and right noting if the leg also rotates. Let the right leg rest. Repeat the same assessment on the left knee. Watch the infant rest. Please watch the video below and consider the following questions while conducting the assessment:

- Does the infant's leg flop with no response? Now, touch or pick up the knees, not to bend, but to rotate gently through the mid-leg.
- Does there seem to be a difference between the right side and the left side?
- Does one side or both sides of the child's body seem not to rotate?
- Does some or all of the infant's body appear to be stiff or floppy?
- Does the infant startle or panic?

If you have answered yes to any of these questions, please place a "1" under the legs/knees section of the Newborn Movement Assessment™ Evaluation Sheet. Please follow-up with your pediatrician immediately if you have any medical concerns.

FEET/ANKLES

INTRODUCTION TO THE FEET/ANKLES

The ankles are good indicators of a body's overall relationship to movement and locomotion.

ASSESSMENT DIRECTIONS FOR THE FEET/ANKLES

Gently touch or pick up the ankles, not to bend, but to rotate gently the foot around the leg. Watch the infant rest. Please watch the video below and consider the following questions while conducting the assessment:

- Does the infant's foot just flop with no response?
- Does the infant's foot seem stiff, straight or hard to bend and rotate?
- Does there seem to be a difference between the right side and the left side?
- Does either one side or both sides of the child's body seem not to rotate?
- Does the infant startle or panic?
- If there are movement concerns, is there rotation in each toe?

If you have answered yes to any of these questions, please place a "1" under the feet/ankles section of the Newborn Movement Assessment™ Evaluation Sheet. Please follow-up with your pediatrician immediately if you have any medical concerns.

Newborn Movement Assessment™
Evaluation Worksheet

• • •

Birth Evaluation

PLEASE ENTER A "1" FOR each of the following birth experiences. If you had a natural childbirth with no other intervention, please skip to the following section.

Types of Childbirth	
Natural Childbirth	
Induced Delivery	
Forceps Delivery	
Use of Vacuum Extraction	

Medicated Childbirth	
Epidural Block	
Pudendal Block	
Spinal Block	
Caudal Block	

Rotation Evaluation

Please enter the following scores:
0 = Rotation and symmetry observed
1 = Lack of rotation or asymmetry observed

Rotation	
Head	

Rotation: Left Side	
Shoulder	
Arms/Elbows	
Wrists/Hands	
Pelvis	
Spine	
Chest	
Legs/Knees	
Feet/Ankles	

Surgical Childbirth	
Cesarean Birth	
General Anesthesia	

Hospitalization (Enter Amount of Days)	
Days in Hospital (NICU)	
Surgery	
Phototherapy	

Medical Assessments	
Diagnosis	
Other Medical Concerns	

FINAL BIRTH SCORE	
TOTAL	

Rotation: Right Side	
Shoulder	
Arms/Elbows	
Wrists/Hands	
Pelvis	
Spine	
Chest	
Legs/Knees	
Feet/Ankles	

FINAL ROTATION SCORE	
TOTAL	

TOTAL ROTATION SCORE	
Final Birth Score	
Final Rotation Score	
TOTAL	

Newborn Movement Assessment™
Scoring System and Implications

• • •

THE NEWBORN MOVEMENT ASSESSMENT™ EVALUATION Worksheet serves to provide the criteria necessary to properly assess your newborn and effectively guide the initiation of a Movement Lesson™. Please take a moment to review your Newborn Movement Assessment™ score. Review your infant's birth history and make sure that you have not missed any events pertinent to the assessment. Reflect on how you can offer purposeful touch to encourage your infant's development. Look at your infant's quality of rotation and consider the following questions:

- Do the words 'stiff' or 'difficult' come to mind?
- Was rotation difficult to observe in any area of your infant's body?
- Was 'unresponsive' or 'I can't tell' part of your vocabulary?

Make a note of these possible thoughts and put them aside. If there are still uncertainties associated with your assessment, please review the video on how to do a Newborn Movement Assessment™ with a child suffering from birth trauma as well as the assessment video for a child with a typical birth history located at www.newbornmovementassessment.com.

SCORES

- **Low Risk (0 – 5)**
  A score between 0 and 5 indicates that your newborn is likely presenting with typical developmental movement patterns and responding properly to your touch. Please feel free to initiate gentle healthy touch as you continue to bond with your child.

- **Slight Risk (5 – 10)**

  A score between 5 and 10 indicates some concerns regarding the ability to move and/or react to stimuli. Start by applying a Movement Lesson™ and initiating a gentle healthy touch during bonding activities and play. Reassess your infant within a week and note if the rotation scores have improved or remain unchanged. Please continue to review these notes on a regular basis with your pediatrician.

- **Moderate Risk (10 – 15)**

  A score between 10 and 15 indicates that your newborn may be at risk for milestone achievements. Start by applying a Movement Lesson™ and initiating a gentle healthy touch on a daily basis, one to two times per day for a period of fifteen minutes to an hour. Reassess your infant on a weekly basis to note any changes in rotation and development. Please continue to review these notes on a regular basis with your pediatrician.

- **High Risk (15 +)**

  A score of 15 or higher indicates your newborn requires a pediatrician's examination and possible additional specialist referrals. During and after hospitalization, start applying a Movement Lesson™ and initiating a gentle healthy touch on a daily basis, for a period of fifteen minutes to an hour. Reassess your infant on a weekly basis to note any rotation and development. Please continue to review these notes on a regular basis with your pediatrician.

The Newborn Movement Assessment™ is not intended to be a substitute for the medical advice of physicians. The reader should regularly consult a physician in matters relating to their infant's health, particularly with respect to any symptoms that may require diagnosis or medical attention.

Touch and Movement

· · ·

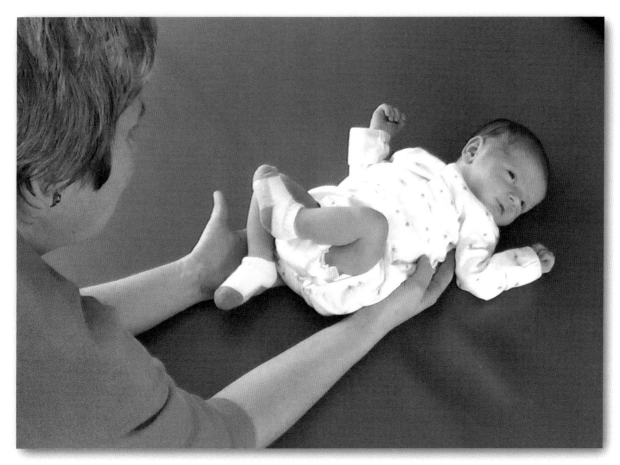

Newborn Movement Assessment™ Basics of Touch

• • •

THE POSSIBILITY OF TOUCH, WITH a sense of wonder and commitment, is very powerful. The more that you touch your baby with an ease of movement, the more that the baby will have an ease of movement. The more that you touch, the more movement possibilities the baby will have. It is that simple.

We usually see the act of touching someone as an emotion or the creation of an emotional response. We know that if we stroke our fingers through our child's hair, we think or hope we are creating a sensation of love and commitment. Through my work creating Movement Lesson™, I have designed a technique to get a responsive touch that includes rotation. When you touch anyone's system, specifically a newborn's, with a gentle, rotational touch, they suddenly have a way of moving that was not possible moments before.

When applying the principles of a Movement Lesson™, you evoke a responsive touch. The application of a gentle touch applied with rotation, allows a system to act or feel as if they are doing the movement. Your touch is so gentle that no force or stress will cause an emotional response. In other words, if I hurt you, you will not want me to do it again, or you will become protective and not be open to learning new experiences. If I suggest or whisper something to you in a pleasant manner, you will be open to a new learning experience. Since a newborn is now reacting to a stimulus, his body will integrate rotation and developmental movement patterns. During a Movement Lesson™, your baby will start to move and develop before your eyes, despite any prior traumas to his systems. Even a baby presenting with a genetic condition and known developmental complications or delays, can respond to your touch and improve movement, creating new neuropathways within minutes of the application. The human brain wants to learn from its surroundings even if there is damage to vital organ function(s). A Movement Lesson™ shows a system that it can respond to the stimulus you provide.

Take a moment and review your Newborn Movement Assessment™ score sheet. Review the birth history and make sure that you have not missed any events pertinent to the assessment. Reflect on how you can offer purposeful touch to encourage your baby's movements. Look at your baby's quality of rotation. Do words like 'stiff' or 'difficult' come to mind? Was rotation difficult to observe in any area of your baby's body? Was 'unresponsive' or 'I can't tell' part of your vocabulary? Make a note of these possible thoughts and put them aside. If you are still not sure, review the video on how to do a Newborn Movement Assessment™ with a child suffering from birth trauma, and the one with a typical birth history. If you did have a typical full-term natural delivery, you may not have concerns about birth trauma or genetics at this time. The knowledge of knowing what to look for in each case provides helpful information on assessing or initiating a Movement Lesson™ with your baby.

Healthy babies naturally respond to touch. Their bodies should have a spring in their muscle tone. They quickly present a natural ability to move in and out of symmetrical and asymmetrical poses as they react to stimuli and increase their cognitive awareness. As a baby increases his ability to know his body and environment, he will have more options to react. Simply showing your baby one new way to process through touch starts a wonderful chain-reaction of movement possibilities. As you work with your baby, you will be complementing their bodies by doing similar movements. The same love that a parent has when caring for their baby's basic needs is the same love that initiates a gentle touch for a Baby Movement Lesson™.

An infant's central nervous system can change immediately and in various mathematical ways through the process of touch. The ideal touch is to use your fingers, hands, and arms in such a way that a baby cannot sense where their central nervous system ends and yours begins. Most people rely only on their eyes for a movement evaluation and neglect the greater amount of information that is receivable through a subtle touch. Be open to the wealth of information that is about to unfold through your baby's response to your touch, as if reading a book for the very first time. The ability to touch with rotation is adding natural movement patterns for the baby, creating new neuropathways. As your system guides their body through successful developmental movement patterns, their brains develop as if they were initiating the responsive action. This simple act opens the door to typical development.

FEATURES OF TOUCH IN A MOVEMENT LESSON

The Newborn Movement Assessment™ offers a gentle method of touch. This slow and gentle method of touch will compel the human mind to pay attention and enhance cognitive brain development. Imagine yourself standing in a large, loud room with hundreds of people talking around you. You do not want to be there and I come up and yell at you to solve a math problem. I do not know if I would get an answer, but if I did, I doubt whether your answer would be correct. Now imagine that I snuggled in behind you, slid my hands around your waist, and whispered in your ear, "Chocolate?". Do you think you would say yes to me? The principles of approach are universal and are especially true with your baby.

Touch with Wonder: Touching with a sense of wonder and inquisitiveness is very powerful. The more that you touch an infant with an ease of movement, the more an infant will have an ease of movement. The more that you touch an infant with natural movement patterns, the more natural movement patterns the infant will have. The same love that a parent has when caring for their infant's basic needs is the same love that initiates a gentle touch for a Baby Movement Lesson™.

Touch with Gentleness: An infant's central nervous system can change immediately and in various remarkable ways through the process of touch. Touch is the most important stimulus in order for the brain to begin to learn and organize information from its environment. The ideal touch is to use your fingers, hands, and arms in such a way that an infant cannot sense where their body ends and yours begins.

Touch with Rotation: The simple act of rotation is the foundation for optimal movement in the human body. The ability to touch with rotation creates and/or increases the body's ability to oppose gravity. The ability to touch with rotation effectively encourages natural movement patterns in an infant and stimulates new neuropathways. Since an infant only learns by reacting to stimuli and you, the parent or professional, are the stimulus providing a specific, gentle, rotational touch, you now have the ability to influence the rest of your infant's life. This simple act opens the door to typical development.

Touching without Intent: For most of us, touch is primarily associated with intent. There is a notable difference in touching someone with the intent of changing them versus touching someone with a sense of curiosity and exploration. It is not about touching a specific body part or a particular point on the body. Feel how your infant moves, not whether she is moving to your touch. An infant only moves in a way that is easiest for his system. They have no capability to purposely move or control their muscles or skeletal system in order to have their needs met. They do not think to themselves, "If I could move my head a little more to the right then I could latch on to my mother". In that same movement conversation, a mother is trying to nurse her crying child, not because of colic, but possibly because the infant is unable to move his body to that side of his mother.

Possible Observations through Touch

Most people rely only on their eyes for a movement evaluation and neglect the significant amount of information that can be gained through a subtle touch.

Tonus: Tonus is a state of tension in muscle tissue that facilitates its response to stimulation. When you touch someone, his or her system should touch you back. The feeling of touch might feel similar to touching rising dough. As you touch the dough and press in with a slight indentation, and then, release your touch, you will watch as the dough springs back out.

Temperature: Feel or observe any changes in temperature throughout the body. Newborns are more sensitive to temperature changes than adults. Therefore, movement can be drastically different in an infant's body due to inflammation, infection, exposure to weather, or tissue trauma from internal or external causes.

Learning Touch

. . .

Being with your baby is a wonderful feeling. Being responsible for your infant's progression by helping him move and respond is the act of a loving parent and caretaker. Take a moment and view the video on "touch". As you apply what you have learned, you will observe immediate changes in your baby and be amazed by their response. Watch the video now, located at www.newbornmovementassessment.com, as I talk you through this tender process.

You will need the following supplies: a bottle of water, a wine glass, a bowl of water and a plate. A newborn baby is about 85% water weight and typically, they do not have muscles that are engaged in an action, so their bodies are quite responsive to touch.

- Pick up your bottle of water. Notice that with a small touch the water in the bottle has a substantial reaction. Place the bottle down and pick up the glass of water. Notice the reaction of the water. Place the glass down. Now pick up the bowl of water and notice the reaction of the water. Place the bowl down.

- Let's explore the bowl. Place your open hands with the back of the hand facing down, and gently make contact with the bowl through your fingers. Think of the bowl as a vessel as you lift the bowl into the palms of your hands. Make a purposeful movement to slosh the water in the bowl. Next, let the water find its stillness. Now, touch the bowl with the intention of moving the bowl around the water. Take a moment, keeping the water still. This is a different concept: trying not to move the water, but instead, moving the bowl around the water. Notice that you are starting to move your hands with a rotational touch as you move the bowl around the water. Take a moment to play and attempt to slosh the water and then go back to moving the bowl around the water. Place the bowl down.

- Let's pick up the wine glass of water placing the stem of the glass in your fingers. The importance of a stemware glass helps you feel and understand the process of balance, counterbalance, counter rotation, and gravity. Work with the wine glass as you did with the bowl of water, moving the glass around the water. Take a moment to notice as you move the glass to the right, the stem of the glass

27

counters to the left. For every action that you take with the bowl of the glass, the stem of the glass has an equal and opposite reaction. These are the principles of balance and counterbalance. Place your fingers on the stem as you get more comfortable with playing with the glass. Continue with slow gentle movements as you move the glass around the water. Notice that the glass is starting to feel top heavy in relationship to the water. Place the glass on the table.

- Take a moment to play with the bowl of water and see if your touch has become easier.

- Now, pick up the wine glass from the base. Slowly start to move the glass around the water. Notice that you need to do this with more concentration on counter rotation, balance, and counterbalance. This is because the effects of gravity or the feeling of heaviness at the top of the glass is part of the conversation of movement rather that tilting an object around the water. Play as you move the glass around the water in this position. Put the glass down.

- Place the plate in the palm of your hand on your fingertips. Notice how the plate feels in your hand. Notice the feeling of balance in your hands through the plate. Most people believe that balance is only through the inner ear, but the relationship to movement, balance, and counterbalance is throughout our bodies. Try to keep the plate still as your fingers start to move around the plate. If the bowl is not too heavy, place it on the plate and begin to move the bowl around the water. Play with this until you are comfortable placing the glass on the plate. Move the glass around the water without the glass moving or sliding on the plate. Place the plate down and pick up the bowl and play with the principles of touch and movement that I will show you in video…

Do you see how gentle your touch is as you work with these objects? If you grab the bowl, it is difficult not to disturb the water's movement. When you hold the bowl or glass, did you notice that you were a part of the object and the water was calm and responding around your movements? These are uncomplicated aspects of working with your baby's movement responses.

Initiating Gentle Healthy Touch

• • •

THE NEWBORN MOVEMENT ASSESSMENT™ IS not intended to be a substitute for the medical advice of physicians. The reader should regularly consult a physician in matters relating to their infant's health, particularly with respect to any symptoms that may require diagnosis or medical attention.

Please watch the following video, located at www.newbornmovementassessment.com, before you proceed with a Newborn Movement Assessment™

HEAD

OVERVIEW OF THE HEAD

The head contains key aspects in the development of the sub-senses. During the first three months, the sub-senses are more critical to development than the topical senses. Before an infant's eyes start to open, they are moving and reacting to the stimuli surrounding them. The sinus cavities generate a key feature in the development of balance and spatial awareness. As the eyes are closed and the head rolls around to the mother and father, the mucus in the nasal cavities and the eye sockets start to synchronize movements as a system. If there is an issue with other senses, it will become apparent in the movement of the head. Offering an infant the same attention from your left and right hand is also important as they are navigating in their new world. You can apply these principles with your infant the moment they are born by using a gentle bonding touch.

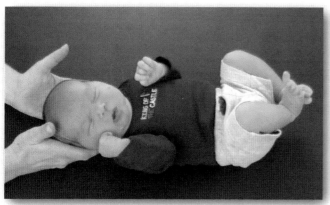

MOVEMENT LESSON BASICS FOR THE HEAD

Simply touch your infant's head in a soft manner without actually holding their head. Place your hands, backside down, next to the side of their head. With the tips of your fingers at the base of the head, gently touch to see how the head responds to the right and to the left. Now gently cup their head into your hands as if you are holding a rose bud. The touch that I am teaching is as soft as if you are touching butter without leaving your fingerprint. Watch the following video as I talk you through these movements:

ADDITIONAL REMARKS ON THE HEAD

Another important movement occurs as the mother is nursing the infant. Most professionals talk about the action of sucking as providing future oral motor skills that are required for talking. As the infant eats, breathes, and moves around the mother, he is learning the movement of coming forward to the breast. This is one of the first experiences in which an infant learns to overcome his system in order to incorporate balance and counterbalance in the opposition of gravity. An infant who is bottle-fed still needs to incorporate these same movements.

SHOULDERS

OVERVIEW OF THE SHOULDERS

Movement in the shoulders will complement the opposite movement in an infant's pelvis. A baby's first reaction should be seen through the shoulders and the pelvis in a synchronized manner. As the baby learns to roll over to tummy time and presents on all fours, this horizontal initiation of counterbalance shows up as it learns airplane and crawling. The vertical presentation shows up as a toddler raises a glass to their face or raises their arms up to be picked up.

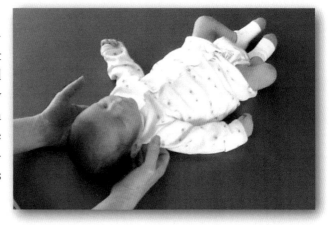

MOVEMENT LESSON BASICS FOR THE SHOULDERS

As your baby is lying down, the simple act of placing your fingers under their shoulders is a Movement Lesson™. The width of your fingers is enough movement to initiate a change. In a soft slow manner, as if the child was crawling or swimming, and with a light lift with rotation, move the right shoulder towards the left shoulder or pelvis. After doing this movement several times, repeat the lesson with the left shoulder. The movements are slow and soft as if you are thinking of a small boat in water.

Additional Remarks

The shoulders should be able to react and counter the movements of breathing, nursing and rolling over. When your baby is one-month old, she should be able to lift up her arms through the shoulder and over the head as they present in lying down. A baby that presents via a C-section has a greater tendency to have less movement through the shoulders and upper body. All movements through the shoulders increase your baby's movement vocabulary.

Arms/Elbows

Overview of the Arms/Elbows

A baby's ability to move his arms and elbows is the initial set up for extension throughout their bodies. As his arms go up and down, he is acquiring large movement patterns based on the opposition to gravity.

Movement Lesson Basics for the Arms and Elbows

As with the spine, a Movement Lesson™ focusing on the arms can be done in any position. As your infant lies in your arms, gently place your fingers around his elbow as if you are picking up a strawberry and are curiously looking at it. Allow his hands to move about as you introduce this movement to the brain. The simple act of rotating the elbow down to your lap and up to a half position or horizontal position is one way an infant gains the sensation of movement which is separate from the activity of the shoulder. If an infant's arms are stiff or floppy, it is an early detector of concern. While using the same 'strawberry hold', you can also introduce a rotation that is similar to gently opening up an upside down bottle of water.

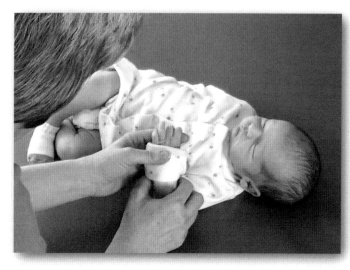

Additional Remarks

Movement through the arms and elbows is just as important as movement through the legs and knees. The initial rotation when a baby first touches breast tissue for feeding is the initiation of standing. The response they receive from this stimulus is the first movement of pushing and going away from an object. Just as you, an adult, goes into standing, your feet approach the floor and your head moves away from your feet.

Wrists/Hands

Overview of the Hands

Watching a newborn's hands slip in and out of yours is a remarkable life experience. The knowledge that one day these five fingers might hold a paintbrush, drive a car or take your hand is wonderful thoughts. This little hand of twenty-seven bones will soon be a gateway to many topical senses and developmental movement patterns. Using your thumb and pointer finger is enough to begin stimulation with a gentle touch and rotation.

Movement Lesson Basics for the Hands

Place your thumb on one side of the wrist and the pointer or middle finger on the other side. With almost no movement on your part, feel the wrist glide within your fingers. As you move your baby's fingers to the chest, imagine the eventual ability to bring food or an object to his mouth. As you move his fingers towards the midsection, imagine that he is learning how to bring his hands to the floor to crawl. If there is any resistance or lack of response, do not use force. Maintain a gentle, healthy touch with rotation.

Move your fingers down into the palm of his hands and continue the same gliding motion as you feel the palm move and in and out of your hand. Notice how his wrists can bend up and down around his hands. They will want to move in and out of your fingers like a little marsupial. These movements will be involuntary as they are simply responding to your stimulus of touch.

Additional Remarks

I do not use lotions or oils during a Movement Lesson™; however a perfect time to do so is when you are bathing or holding your infant. Other stimuli variations can be found in cloth and textures from your clothing or his bedding. This is only the beginning of the many ways to use touch with your infant before he is able to hold an object on his own.

As your infant grows, his hands can be a telltale sign for concerns with development. Knowing your baby's abilities and inabilities is crucial to understanding his milestone developments.

During an infant's first few weeks, the tendency for them to be more spastic and exhibit fisted hands is greater. Do not be surprised at sudden jerks or contractions.

SPINE

OVERVIEW OF THE SPINE

A Movement Lesson™ focusing on the infant's spine and chest cavity can be done while the infant is cradled to your chest or lying on a blanket. Holding your infant close to your own body is a wonderful, bonding experience. This is especially true when using an adaptation of the 'Joey Hold', commonly done with premature infants.

MOVEMENT LESSON BASICS FOR THE SPINE

Gently place your infant's chest against your chest. At the same time, place your other hand across the infant's pelvis. During any Movement Lesson™, there is never an occasion to touch the spine directly. Place your fingers, not on the spine but to the side of the spine. Start your gentle, rotational touch at the top of the back, repeating the process down the spine every quarter of an inch. As you bring awareness to their spine, incorporate a slight twist with the hand that is across his pelvis. This is helping to create and enforce a gentle counterbalance and rotation through the spine and pelvis.

To create this same movement pattern on a table, place your infant in a side-lying position. At the same time, place your other hand across the infant's pelvis. Place your fingers, not on the spine but to the side of the spine. Create a motion that looks like you are about to play the piano, and gently touch the top position of the side of the spine. Start your gentle, rotational touch at the top of the spine, repeating the process down the spine every quarter of an inch. As you bring awareness to the infant's spine, incorporate a slight twist with your hand that is across their pelvis. This is helping to create and enforce a gentle counterbalance and rotation through the spine and pelvis.

ADDITIONAL REMARKS

The spine needs wonderful gentle motions that reflect movement throughout a baby's body. A stiff spine will be accompanied by a stiff body. A floppy spine will be seen in a non-responsive infant. The health of the spine is crucial because it lead to carrying their system through life.

CHEST

OVERVIEW OF THE CHEST

Gentle chest work can be done while your infant is lying on his back or in your arms. Stimulating the chest will help your infant develop various movement milestones including breathing and crossing the mid-line. If you decide to bottle feed rather that nurse your infant, you may want to consider chest work. When you are nursing, the infant's chest cavity has an increased opportunity to learn to breathe more efficiently, and rotate from the left and right positions. An infant fed from a bottle or neonatal gastric (NG) tube, has fewer opportunities to experience movement from the left and right positions.

MOVEMENT LESSON BASICS FOR THE CHEST

With one hand to the side of the spine and the other hand to the side of the center of the chest (not directly on but around the sternum or chest bone), initiate a gentle, healthy touch as if you were sliding or moving to the side. At the same time, the hand on the back is countering the same movement. Watch the video as I talk through these movements. Do not try to apply the tempo of this touch to your infant's breathing as he breathes at a much faster rate than an adult. It is not a form of CPR but a way of showing the chest cavity how to move and twist around the spine.

ADDITIONAL REMARKS

The simple act of the breast bone (sternum) being able to twist and cross mid-line precede the ability to sit, stand and tie our shoes. We are taught that it is an important milestone to cross over the chest with the arms, but for a baby with a stiff or non-responsive chest cavity this is an impossible task.

PELVIS

OVERVIEW OF THE PELVIS

Every time you change your infant's diaper, a wonderful opportunity arises to work with his pelvis. Changing this routine by pulling the tabs in to close the diaper, you can rotate the pelvis from side to side to meet the tab.

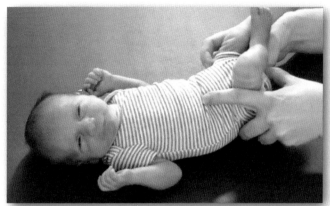

Movement Lesson Basics for the Pelvis

As you scoop or cup your hands under a diapered bottom, leave each hand under each pelvis. Work with one side with a few gentle lifts. Now initiate gentle lifts on the other side, rising no more than an inch from the surface where the infant is laying. Now, try another new movement. Gently lift one side of the pelvis as you rock or go to the left and then back again. Now gently rock the other side of the pelvis. Imagine a tiny boat rocking back and forth on the water. This is the same motion of going from side to side with your infant, safe in your hands. When you are finished playing with the rocking of the pelvis, you can then work on a gentle roll.

Additional Remarks

Another opportunity to work with your infant's pelvis is during his daily bathing routine. It is perfectly natural to wash and rotate the bottom. Using the same action as you might when apply lotion or a wipe, do this through the right side of the pelvis, and then through the left as you turn your baby through the sit bones.

If you find that your infant startles or seems stiff as you move him through your hands, you need to remember that less is more. As with the bowl of water, the ability to move your child without getting a reaction can be somewhat difficult at first. You are teaching your infant that he can move without a startle. When your infant can move without startling, you can begin introducing gentle rotation into his vocabulary while his system learns to react and move through your hands.

Legs/Knees

Overview Of The Legs/Knees

Working with the knees and legs first is an excellent way to introduce a Movement Lesson™ to your infant. As with all body parts, an alert infant will unconsciously play with the opposition of gravity. A leg/knee movement away from the body will spring back to the pelvis or floor. This is an infant's way of playing by moving away from the lying down position that will eventually lead to walking.

Movement Lesson Basics for the Legs/Knees

As your infant lies comfortably on his back, place yourself at his feet looking at his face. When working with the right leg, place your right hand into the mid-section holding the diaper. Hold the back of the right leg, including the knee. Gently rotate the leg/knee through the pelvis into the leg. Do the same with the left leg. This is similar to the feeling one has when driving a car.

Additional Remarks

A popular concept is mimicking a bicycle in the air, but this is not recommended for an infant as it restricts rotation through the foot and lower leg, and reduces movement throughout the chest cavity. It also limits a baby's ability to spring up and play with the opposition of gravity. Simply by changing your hand position to go under the infant's knees, you can safely perform the same bicycle action. Not only will you get more movement with rotation through the legs, pelvis and chest cavity, your infant will suddenly be able to stretch and contract his legs.

Feet/Ankles

Overview of the Feet/Ankles

My favorite part of the body to work with is the feet. Even though you and I may go to the gym, or move from one place to another, we do little to improve foot function. The feet are the simplest indicator of development. The movement of rotating a heel in and out can tell me if a baby will be able to crawl or side sit. Rather than wait for these milestones to happen naturally, you can begin now to offer different stimuli that will improve their feet and overall body functions.

If you find the feet difficult to manage because they are small and moving around, know that any Movement Lesson™ can be applied while your infant is sleeping. The neurological influence of any Movement Lesson™ can occur whether your infant is awake or asleep.

When your infant is in your arms or on a blanket, take time to observe his feet. It will not be long before they will be interested in walking and running. The feet should be able to flex, jump, stand, slide and walk within a nano second. Enjoy these images and other possibilities as you use the 'strawberry hold' that you learned with the elbows. In this gentle position, simply feel how the heels rotate from side to side. You should notice if the heel of the foot can move around the lower leg. The foot should not consistently move like a windshield wiper. If this happens, be sure you are incorporating Movement Lesson™ into your daily schedule.

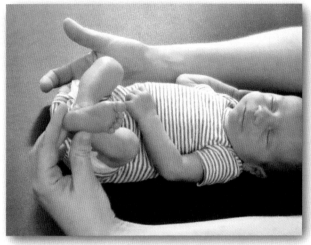

Movement Lesson Basics for the Feet/Ankles

Now gently touch and stimulate each toe. This is especially important if your infant required an IV or had a pulse oximeter around the feet. Initiate a gentle, rotational touch to each toe. As if they were little keys on a typewriter, allow the toe to respond back to your downward touch. Feel free to add the poem, 'This Little Piggy', to each toe. These movements can be incorporated starting from the top or the bottom of the foot.

Additional Remarks

Begin to understand and see your infant's body as a whole and functioning system that quickly seeks to integrate with your gentle touch. An infant's big toe is important to his future ability to walk, run, and balance. The inability of the big toe to walk, run, or balance will increase the strain on the circulatory system. The heart, being the most important part of the circulatory system, is important to the function of all systems. Therefore, when the heart system fails, was it due to the heart or the body's inability to balance? If we continue to address the human body as pieces and parts, we will never realize its complexity as a complete system. The brain is more complex than science acknowledges today. It functions as a response to specific movements and reactions to stimuli, which include the basic laws of physics and mathematics. We still need to offer our newborns a natural environment where they can transition in and out of different movements that provide the stimulus needed for development.

The information contained in this guide offers a window into your infant's brain.
First, you will you have a more accurate view of your baby's well-being. Second, you will be able
to increase your skills when articulating your baby's milestones during his first year. Having this
information available enables you and your professionals to have better insight into your child's
development.

Movement Lesson™

. . .

Principles of a Movement Lesson™

. . .

A Movement Lesson™ is the ability to touch a baby so that he does not know whether he is initiating an action, receiving an action or a response.

A MOVEMENT LESSON™ IS BASED upon the principles of rotation and responsive touch. During a Movement Lesson™, infants will start to move and develop before your very eyes, despite any prior traumas to their systems. Even infants presenting with a genetic condition or known developmental delays will respond to your touch and improve their movement patterns, creating new neuropathways within minutes of the application.

We usually see the act of touching someone as an emotion or the creation of an emotional response. We know that if we stroke our fingers through our child's hair, we think or hope we are creating a sensation of love and commitment. During a Movement Lesson™, the touch is so gentle that no force or stress will cause an emotional response. In other words, if I hurt you, you will not want me to do it again, or you will become protective and not be open to learning new experiences. If I suggest or whisper something to you in a pleasant and suggestive manner, you will be more open to a new learning experience. The application of a gentle touch applied with rotation, allows a system to act or feel as if they are doing the movement. The individual receiving the Movement Lesson™ should be unable to tell whether they are initiating the action, receiving the action, or responding to the action.

When applying the principles of a Movement Lesson™, you are evoking a responsive touch. When you touch anyone's system, specifically a newborn's system, with a gentle, rotational touch, they suddenly have a way of moving that was not possible moments before. This slow and gentle method of touch will compel the human mind to pay attention and enhance cognitive brain development.

MICHELLE TURNER'S THEORY ON MOVEMENT, ROTATION, AND GRAVITY

In the womb, the mother's body produces an environment for the creation of a human being. The amniotic fluid creates a sensation of little gravity, which enables the body to have the ability to expand and grow in all directions with an equal force. Since there is no dominant organ function, as in breathing, the lack of movement and expansion without rotation creates an environment for optimal growth and development. Nature has intended that at approximately 38 to 40 weeks, movement patterns start to change within a mother to prepare the system for delivery. The typical delivery happens when a baby brings itself into a head down position to prepare for a vaginal birth. At the same time, contractions start to present an external force stimulating the baby's central nervous system and preparing the body for the true sense of gravity that is present outside of the womb. As this process continues, contractions and the severity of the contractions continue in greater frequency. The mother will dilate and in most cases, the sack will break which ends this 'non-gravitational' sensation and brings the baby through the vaginal canal for his first breath.

My theory of rotation includes the following statement. The **organization of human body functions is due to the principle of the opposition of gravity.** The current belief is that gravitational force keeps us on the ground. If an apple falls from a tree, it will strike the ground with the same speed or momentum as a brick. The conclusion is that gravitational force is the same for everyone. We know there is 14.7 pounds of gravitational force per square inch on every aspect of our body. However, the organization of the brain does not succumb to gravity. It does not have the ability to move or roll around due to the constant pressure of gravity

Looking at the opposition of gravity from another aspect, one does not walk down the hallway with your conscious mind saying, "Don't fall, don't fall". Our thought process suddenly becomes very limited because the system is surviving rather than processing the ability to learn and function. For most of us, the act of walking is just that, walking or moving through space. When rotation is non-existent or traumatized, your conscious mind consumes itself with not falling. Why? In this moment, the neuropathways of your brain have lost their relationship to gravity. The rotation or the ability to rotate allows the brain and central nervous system to work within the law of opposing gravity.

Through my studies and experiences with special needs children, I realized that they do not have a proper awareness of rotation throughout their system. No matter the diagnosis, these children have a different quality of life. The aspect of rotation became an obsession as I looked at minute movement patterns and their relationship to rotation. I realized my touch and approach to Movement Lesson was different because I included the force or presence of rotation and torque in my application of gentle touch and movement. I was reading a book on Einstein to my son Graham about the aspects of leaving Earth's gravitational force as the space shuttle rotated into space. My conclusion is that we have been looking at the human body the wrong way. Though it is true that we do not float away due the Earth's gravitational force, the central nervous system bases itself on the principle of the opposition of gravity.

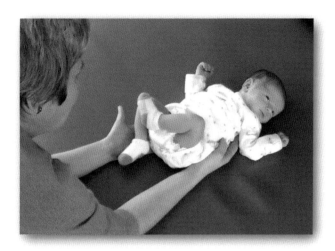

How a Baby Learns

Learning from Movement

A new and developing brain only learns from the ability to react to stimulus. A moving baby creates small, yet crucial, responses to stimuli that initiate the cerebral functions that science can barely explain today. To execute any movement that a newborn experiences, requires some degree of rotation. **This rotation not only influences, but is required to create neuropathways in a newborn's brain.** This movement formula is not the same as the cognitive processing in an adult brain. We tend to use the fully developed adult brain as a reference for independent locomotion, intellect, and emotions that come after movement. The ability to not only acknowledge these movement patterns but to influence them as your infant is responding to its environment is crucial in early development.

Take a step back and visualize the formation of a developing brain as a newly formatted hard drive with very basic functions that cannot perform simple or reactive tasks until applications and codes are applied. Your smart phone or iPad is not very interesting until you load some apps that we can use in our day-to-day activities. My smart phone can have more possibilities and be smarter than I am because if I do not know to look for the available information, I cannot react to the data. The human brain is very similar to these processing skills. The actions that you and I might take for granted, such as heart functioning and breathing can be milestones to an infant who cannot breathe on his own. An infant's brain is not only a receptive vessel but can grasp an infinite amount of movements in nanoseconds. During the initial movements of a newborn, the brain immediately 'files' all of these events that are happening and begins the complex task of cross categorizing through the topical senses (touch, sight, sound, taste and smell) and also the body's sub-senses (balance, counter balance, rotation, gravity, temperature, spatial proportions, and acceleration). The varieties of senses that our body has the capacity to work with are similar to tags on the computer. The larger the number of tags that I have attached to my videos allows you to find specifically what you need when searching for 'movement', 'hip', 'cerebral palsy', 'non-alternative', or 'non-surgical'. The same goes for the human brain when reaching for a spoon. If balance and counterbalance are not something that the brain has experienced in relation to the central nervous system, then the body is limited in its availability to pick up the spoon.

---

balance: noun
Balance is the result of a number of body systems moving and working together in space.

---

counterbalance: noun
a weight balancing another weight; an equal movement or weight acting in opposition.

The five senses we learn in childhood are what professionals believe are the keys to development. When a child presents with a deficit in one or more of these areas of touch, sight, sound, taste, and smell, a diagnosis of a Sensory Integration Disorder, a Sensory Processing Disorder, or a Multi-Sensory Deficit Disorder may be given. When a baby, hours old, hears a noise, he turns his head as a response. I refer to this as reacting to stimuli because babies do not know that they are hearing, seeing, touching, tasting, or smelling.

The breakthrough I am sharing is the notation and development of touch around a baby's sub-senses. We know that in typical development, a child reacting to light or sound on its right side should show a typical response of tilting the head and/or looking to the right. Picture this same image, and as the child reacts to a right sided stimulus, a healthy system will have an equal and opposite counter reaction on the lower left side. The act of balance and counterbalance through the pelvis creates a body or central nervous system response that enables a baby to 'look' to the right. When an infant is unable to balance and counterbalance through the pelvis, due to a restriction, then he cannot react to the stimulus. If the inability to react to stimulus continues, the same baby will have a life of short-term to long-term complications.

TRADITIONAL OR TOPICAL SENSES

- Hearing
- Taste
- Smell

- Touch
- Sight

NON-TRADITIONAL OR SUB-SENSES

- Balance
- Counterbalance
- Gravity
  - ° Succumb
  - ° Opposition
- Rotation
- Temperature
- Acceleration
- Pain
- Proprioception – kinesthetic sense
- Spacial Orientation

Realizing that the same newborn that cannot turn his head without physical intervention, which includes rotation, will also not be able to roll over, play in tummy time, sit up to the right, or have the ability to walk and run with ease. Most therapists believe that this is the time to start services. I have discovered that low tone and high tone infants can milestone if they have rotation. Since it is a fact that muscle function alone will not get you up off the floor, the most effective solution is to initiate rotation to change movement function, not muscle function. When our skeletal systems know how to react as nature has intended, then our muscles will have the ability to do the same.

As a brain develops, it continues to learn and react to stimuli throughout the body. Counterbalance is not as obvious in a developed adult brain when the head turns toward a noise. The adult way of processing movement is to use topical senses to SEE a baby reaching for a ball. The use of only topical senses is naive and gives a limited option on the way we view movement. As I see and feel a baby moving through space, they are not only reacting to the stimulus (the ball), but this also prompts continuous feedback to their sub-senses. A baby unable to move through space, due to restriction, birth trauma, and/or genetics, may not be capable of playing and developing around these principles. Understanding the movement relationship between the topical senses and the sub-senses can benefit the bonding experience between parent and child by using specific and productive stimulus, which then increases the aptitude for movement and cognitive development.

My theory negates the current theory of balance, which refers to the inner ear as the processing center for regulating basic functions. While it is true that if you or I suffered a trauma to the inner ear and/

or the brain, we would immediately show a decrease in our ability to balance. The damage to this part of the body has drastic effects on balance but is only one part of the system. I refer to this as the sub-sense of balance. Each part of the body should be able to exhibit these sub-senses as it moves and reacts to stimuli.

The Newborn Movement Assessment

Birth and Development

The wonders of birth and development never cease to amaze me. Whether you are touching your baby for the first time or have the privilege, of doing this every day, the act of touching another human being is a marvel. The complexities of the body's systems and their integration will be clear as we examine each area of a baby's body. This is a perfect moment to look at a human being as a living and functioning system. The aspect of working with a baby has become so natural that I developed an acute sense of sight and touch. The videos of infants and toddlers on my website are there to help parents enhance their infant's development. I can recognize a language or a movement vocabulary developing throughout another person's body or system. Through the Newborn Movement Assessment™, not only will you begin to understand this natural language of movement, you will also gain knowledge of how to develop this language into new and purposeful developmental movement patterns.

Most people do not realize that they already possess and understand the language of movement. It does not take rocket science to know that if I arrive home late; find my teenage son with his arms crossed and the "look" on his face, to know the direction of our conversation. The more time I spend giving a Movement Lesson™, the more I increase my own movement vocabulary. Because of this, I have a quicker response and am able to influence a baby's movement vocabulary through my touch. Since a baby only learns by reacting to stimulus and you, the parent or professional, are the stimulus providing a specific, gentle, rotational touch, you now have the ability to influence the rest of your baby's life. Using the principles within this guide, you will influence your baby and his system as he learns, reacts, or responds to your touch.

If a childbirth does not go as planned, the Newborn Movement Assessment™ will determine if their system found aspects of the delivery as traumatic. A baby will not show any movement, react in anyway, and will not progress in development if a reaction is difficult or hurts. Their central nervous system processes this learned experience as unavailable or what you and I know as 'can't'. A baby's reaction to stimuli is in contrast to that of adult cognitive behavior. A mother must care for her children despite the fact that her back hurts or she is sick. A father might muscle up and throw a ball even though he threw his shoulder out weeks ago. In contrast, it is critical to note that an infant or toddler is smarter that we are and will not be able to respond if any movement is difficult or hurts them.

Have you ever had an IV in your writing arm? You should be able to write or type with a needle in your wrist. The IV is only a couple of ounces. Your pain level is not as great as when the original needle was inserted. However, for some reason, your system finds it difficult to write your name. A baby, who cannot lift his arm when he hears a noise or is limited because of an IV, a harness, or a swaddle cloth, will be unable to file a successful sequence of movements in their brain. When you are able to feel and/or recognize trauma in a baby's system, not only is it a powerful position to be in, but you can acknowledge the limitations and then influence a successful movement through a gentle touch.

Empowering parents with the ability to look at their child with the belief that something could be wrong is knowledge. The Newborn Movement Assessment gives parents the ability to redirect potential outcomes using specific and easy tools for development. You can set up a phone or video camera to record your thoughts and observations as you evaluate your child. You have movement awareness as you touch your baby in a manner that gives instant feedback. This enables you to have knowledge about their cognitive development and health. The simple act of rotation is the foundation for optimal movement in the human body. If I were to ask someone to lie down on their back on the floor, or in the comfort of their bed, and then tell them to stand up without using any rotation, most people could not do it. The realization is that if a baby does not present with functional rotation, he then cannot react to stimulus and would therefore begin to succumb to the effects of gravity.

No one sets out in life to do something perfect on the first try. After the birth of our baby, we joyfully watch as our infant initiates wonderful, yet seemingly random, movements. Our infant graduates to imitation and purposeful play through thousands of variations and trials. These movements, done without any conscious objectives, are some of the most important milestones your child can and should exhibit. Since we learn through purposeful play, the general view is to note changes in important milestones such as sitting and crawling. By the age of three months, all of the skills from learned developmental movement patterns are established. The simple, and yet complex act of writing this book was set in motion at the beginning of learning: using fine motor skills to slowly go upright, hold an object, scribble, imitate, and write. This imagery goes a step further as we learn our ABC's, develop language, and learn cursive writing. If an eager parent tells their two-year-old they are about to endure five plus years of work, before writing their first paragraph in cursive, the essence of play and the joy of learning is lost. This is apparent to many, because as we age we stop learning, not because of intelligence, but because the love of learning and enthusiasm for it is gone. Movement allows cognitive functions to continue to develop, mature, and evolve throughout life.

Movement may be limited or non-existent because of random events or trauma to the central nervous system. These events tend to create alternate developmental movements that can limit or redirect neuropathways. A baby's neurological function thrives from movement, and is a requirement for growth. The establishments of small delicate moves that a baby experiences with his body are early system responses that may lead to piano recitals, Saturday soccer games, and their school performances. All of our learned human functions derive from happy accidents and random movements that turn into sophisticated actions and events. There is concern that infants who begins life with trauma, and cannot oppose gravity or experience random movements may have limitations that affect their development later in life. Infants, who begin life with trauma, cannot oppose gravity or experience random movements. There is concern that as they age these limitations may affect development.

It is my belief that it is crucial to help a baby's nervous system develop a stronger connection to movement before the child displays enough evidence to proceed to a developmental delay and/or autism diagnosis. The Newborn Movement Assessment™ gages where an infant is in relation to their ability to react to stimuli, and therefore increases the ability to achieve developmental movements and cognitive functions.

As we observe an infant slowly bringing its hand up in the air to reach for an object, the fingers open and close while the hand rotates. During this simple act, parents are witnessing the beginnings of touch, depth perception, surface reaction, and eye/hand coordination. In a scenario where that same hand has an IV in its wrist, that typical movement conversation is unable to complete the movement. Imagine if we remove all babies IV's, assess the baby, and he or she immediately receives a Movement Lesson™. This insures that rotation and response are initiated, allowing the brain to develop through increased movement to their system. When we compound those life moments with a compromised system, we limit the child beyond the initial diagnosis. We cannot allow a baby's brain to succumb to areas of developmental concerns and delays due to the inability to respond to developmental movements.

Movement Lesson

The Newborn Movement Assessment™ will continue with videos, guides, apps, and a book to guide you through your infant's first year of life. Information on new ways to incorporate an educational touch into your baby's life will continually be available. By following Newborn Movement Assessment™ on Facebook, you will find and have access to a community involved with infant assessment, growth and development. I am dedicated to helping you and your child develop and grow. Learning about their developmental movement patterns from the first moment of their life or as you learn about various ways to incorporate Movement Lesson™ is already at your fingertips through the video support that I have created.

This guide contains information about the principles used every day at Movement Lesson™. There are over 700 instructional videos available. For additional help, go to www.MovementLesson.com. You will find explanations relating to various developmental movements, with and without complications. You will be able to immediately become involved in every stage of your infant's development.

Becoming a Certified Newborn Movement Assessment™ and Movement Lesson™ Practitioner

• • •

IF YOU ARE INTERESTED IN becoming a Newborn Movement Assessment™ Practitioner and/or a Movement Lesson™ Practitioner, please contact Michelle Turner directly. Certification courses are offered throughout the year in the United States and internationally. By joining this exciting community, you will learn how to help infants from the moment they enter into the world and change the lives of countless children and families. You can learn more about these and other opportunities at www.NewbornMovementAssessment.com and www.MovementLesson.com.

About Michelle Turner and Movement Lesson™

• • •

OUT OF NECESSITY TO HELP her globally delayed child, Michelle Turner, Movement Integration Specialist, created Movement Lesson™ to benefit children throughout the world. Founded in 2009, Movement Lesson™, LLC is a private practice located in Peoria, Arizona, USA, and is dedicated to helping children from ages 0 – 94 achieve increased mobility, pain relief, and optimal health. In contrast to the myriad of conventional therapies, a Movement Lesson™ is a progressive, scientific approach that is based on her theory of the opposition of gravity and principles of movement affecting development. More specifically, a Movement Lesson™ utilizes a unique combination of gentle touch and purposeful movement through the principles of counterbalance and rotation to create an individualized and profoundly effective movement lesson session.

Printed in Great Britain
by Amazon